The Throat-Bird

Afric McGlinchey

SurVision Books

First published in 2024 by
SurVision Books
Dublin, Ireland
www.survisionmagazine.com

Copyright © Afric McGlinchey, 2024

Cover image © Michael Ray, 2024

Design © SurVision Books, 2024

ISBN: 978-1-912963-53-9

This book is in copyright. No part of this publication may be reproduced, stored in a retrieval system, or transmitted in any form or by any means without the prior permission in writing from the publisher.

Acknowledgements

Grateful acknowledgement is made to the editors of the following, in which a number of these poems, or earlier versions of them, originally appeared:

*Bloodstone Review, Cafe Review, Haunted by Cycles of Return (*an *Oxford Climate Change* anthology*), Inkroci, New Contrast, Pedestal, Poethead, Poets Meet Painters anthology, Poetry Ireland Review, Sixteen.*

CONTENTS

Bone	5
Between *before* and *after*	6
Black trees open their wings	8
Ghost birds	10
Elsewhere	12
On changing my mind	13
Bedroom tenant	14
Found – The sycamore shadow rocks and falls	16
Waiting	18
The rapture of daffodils	19
In the solitaries	20
Blue	22
What comes next?	24
The ignorance of fish	25
Sister tides	26
Promising music, then falling silent	27
What sleeps are made of	28
Spiral	29
Black Jack	30
Let us gull	31
Doll	32
The body washed dark	33
Immersion	34
Tumbling	36
Something like air	38

Bone

Once charismatic, a mighty presence,
these past ten years
you've been thinned to a skeleton,
resurrecting memories,
the dog hoarding his bone
Still, you sit at the counter of the party
not wanting anything else
Being alive is all you need
The rending sound of a firing squad
is not the sound you'll hear
You make of tomorrow a blindfold
You are the anthill of rituals,
though yours is a house being torn apart,
the hole in the roof
howling rubble

Between *before* and *after*

> *Nothing is so painful to the human mind*
> *as a great and sudden change*
>   – Mary Shelley

My sister can run for hours
Like an animal, she knows how to hide
She watches what goes on in the valley below,
    people passing on foot
at the base of the mountain,
phone screens
        flashing
   like Lucifer stars

She's gone somewhere high,
          far
from those who decide
    who is unacceptable,
far from   *what* is unacceptable

I can imagine her singing that no one wants death today,
that nobody's going to die
       and her feet feel safe

Want an apple?
       A free ticket?

Offering nonchalance, then accepting
a coffee with her mouth open,
       perhaps her luck
              turning into no one
refusing to let her stay

And that bicycle she's riding
has been given to her and hers
       is the wild spirit
through counties of irregular shapes
Get past the black nights, I wrote in my letter
       You'll find open doors
She'll be wondering what's next

Black trees open their wings

The doors, flung open,
        launch into single high notes

An owl lifts at the punch-line
        What war?

Those leathery gloves
        are a hand to the mouth

Even the frogs have subsided
        to an occasional *gooac*

Now we're listening
        to Three Blind Mice

in various styles, while bats whoosh
        next to our ears

A country of dark canopies,
skimming around the grand piano,
        all our *oh dears*

My father veers into jazz and baroque...
                the end of the end
won't be
        before winter

Ghost birds

No bird calls
The avocados sleepy
        and the heat rising

from the spotted
        furnace
of a ladybird's back

He's staring
        into the shade
of the garden

from flower to flower,
        the way everyone
wants, wants

Out of the chasm-
        deep ruts,
grass bristling

and I follow his eyes,
        to see the huge,
invisible wings,

like thousands
          of minnows,
flimmering

Elsewhere

In a moment of refraction and shadow,
a plane floats overhead,
        delicately as a feather
Egyptian cotton wafts
A train somewhere whistles
        You aren't happy, he tells me,
until you consider yourself
              happy

The afternoon light is falling
        in a diagonal
the length of the floor,
            an arrowed line
        of black gun powder
I follow it, feel him brace for it,
and then I'm migrating, I'm gone
and there's only grief here

On changing my mind

I cannot pretend I understand
the throat-bird
or cursed fears
      that come burning

Song, as birds know, is the solace

But all at once, this silk-flashing
is heaven brought down
      to the eleventh hour
a live bird making light
        of despair

I take to a deep-
      moving lake
and gladness enters
    the late afternoon
        lifting
those old wounds
from my palm

Bedroom tenant

The wonder of this creature
pulling silk from her body, weaving
a crystalline circuitry!

A geometry of starry singularities
which I always leave
untouched

for luck
She is attendant in a corner
calm as a sphinx

And if that bulbous black abdomen
flutters the stomach
what poetry in her hammock

I've never seen a web
half-constructed, left incomplete,
never witnessed the embrace of her prey

From a daylight distance,
admiration is easy
but the dark brings a whistling tremor

heightens her presence
and I wonder if she'll flash
a silver thread

parachute to skin
drop venom
into my open mouth

Found **– The sycamore shadow rocks and falls**

backward, to the shock of plant and animal, child
Read it in the child's face

That bit of green ground
                on the hummock

You'd be quite loaded with hawthorn,
sacred as a white goddess

Three sorts of skink on various rocks
                and in the pond, two minnow,
flakes in the air floating a look

We'd fall asleep in a feeling element,
        full of sweet noises from the barn-bouncers
lifting live larvae and crickets and grain

Fallen pearls on the fringe of a coat
                jabbed shut like a clam

Less than three feet across
                by a hood of rocks,
you gather leaflike lichen – and spy them

They, whom the birds despise, start to cut
        into mud gelded by paraquat,

bare paddocks bordered by a creek

And where the woodmen lop,
trampling down the white-shaken flowers,
The night insects – locusts, cicadas –
                      keep screaming

Waiting

I occupy the shady spaces, thin as pins,
lean like an old tree growing dreamy

At dawn, the pane is a dragonfly wing
and the flowers are on tiptoe

And still, still,
I can't get things out

These particles of cloud and matter
        tasting of salt in the throat

The rapture of daffodils

It's hard to give you
                affection
indifferent as you are
to the encompassing embrace
        or passing caress –
and as for giving presents, well,
I did not particularly
bring you these daffodils
with their wide-open gestures
curtainless feelings –
it's just that I can't forget
that death
                lasts
and lasts

In the solitaries

That quiver of air
              shaking the palm leaves
the moon, tightly roped in
bristling, an egg
                  on the edge

Those last knives of light,
the sky so cold it's like burning,
        wind pushing
into my molecules

The weeks repeating
              their spirals
like the swivel of a wrist

What I miss most –
              the pin-drop
attention of another's gaze

The perilous streets, metal air ticking
          like the dark holes
of all my tomorrows

until I see it: the light
                of the sea
and its roof

crimson
        scissoring the ocean,
lifting the flying fish

Blue

My mama was a vampire squid

Each morning, my arms
        were rivers running toward her
When she smiled, I smiled,
        and the whole house pulsed
with our skip-to-the-kitchen laughter

She always stood, breakfast lit on
        by long fingers
and scooped onto her tongue
I'd leave her some crusts,
        bite-sized, briny, crunchy
She had no plate of her own

One day, *he* turned up, back from abroad,
and I screamed and banged my spoon
Saw through the doorway a man
                in uniform, blue beret

I stared at the derelict snowflakes
floating from the wasteland
      of the ceiling,
felt her voice body to my limbs,
as she whirled back through the door, heaving,
and lifted me high in the air,
her arms, a cat's cradle
          I'd have put to sea in

What comes next?

Crouched on the roof
      you knee up the tiles
          your feet bared
          like your soul

         lisp along
      the top of the ridge
    shrouded
by *what ifs*

The ignorance of fish

A fish swims, unaware of surface danger,
        until its body leaves water
and discovers a burning tide in its bones

For soldiers, the rhythm of *inconvenient truth*
becomes the rhythm of ricochet
                      And it's now
that the body whimpers, the body as a red swell

We are fish sailing through air,
        gulping at all the cloud sirens
wailing on the bare hill

When we were a child, the high hill – covered in trees –
        was a playground
I bite my tongue, swallow the blood

Sister tides

Tide is in, all I see is water
Possession is nine
responses
How do you
judge something?
While we still have furniture,
can't throw out the tides
Yeah, no, just looking
out my window
Today, the sea's
a bit rough, as though it's been hit
recently
You'd swear
previous hurricane warnings
would have been helpful
It's beyond online
Whose response do you want?
Here, you have mountains of water,
the audio of a storm
right through Wednesday, sea
plundering the sea

Promising music, then falling silent

Splintery armfuls
      of the most brazen kind
           send one scurrying
Massive hands move clockwise
      across four cardinals
A wheel is plundered
A horse snorts yes
One groans
This is memory
Or dream
The jets of steam,
      pausing
Scavengers carting away
           redundant people
Here and gone
There and now
The chill, hurrying into grey
Waves swallowing hard,
      burying themselves
at our feet

What sleeps are made of

When flakes of the night's activities
                        float back
to our waking state,
it's like the muffled shock
                        of a secret
unintended for our ears

As if one's shadow, attempting escape,
leaps up, sheer,
                leaving the body

A slab of banditry
where we are governed by the laws
of an alien universe

What's looted later
criss-crosses the architectonics
                of a rubble-strewn city
– that half-wall,
                this slice of a window –
under a shower of meteors

No wonder we sleep for years

Spiral

The children eavesdrop on the spiral stairs,
still as musical statues
The words are murmured, but clear enough
From the skylight, a cloud crosses
like a flung-out sheet

A large room, French doors,
fern plants and a fishbowl
Pigeon-toed, elbows planted on chins
      to hold the weight
of heavy heads, they crane their ears

From the painting, a bull churns the ground,
stirs dust to a mighty blood orange
By dawn, it's been decided
The news of another move pours over them,
like water down a slide

Black Jack

In every dream, I walk out
of the arena, all the way to Torres Novas – but wake
to a death stench, blood whirlpools,
        that battalion of red flags

They say you taste iron when you get speared
And only mosquitoes clap at your *écarté*
            over the muddy Guadalquivir
What the hell's the point?

I'm just a freak-show to these vultures,
and I'll say this: there won't be a mass pilgrimage
           to the frozen relics of bulls!
All I've got to look forward to is that slow, unspeakable kill

So why not? They say you should aim for the navel, spike guts
and gore until the matador bubbles saliva,
like caviar; then head for the peace
            shimmering over the hills

Let us gull

Let's say we're gulls
swooping our
       spyglass

over the turbulent
       onrush,
feverish dreams

       bleeding
into the white noise
of waves

over the dune, the warm hill,
in the absence of wind,
holding its hair-grasses still

and we float in the abeyance
between long dashes
and dots

still – for now – alive-o

Doll

Look at the beach, strewn
        with rubbish and junk,
and that small girl, immersed
in the shallows next to a bucket,
bleached colourless

In her gestures, she offers
        an attitude,
her little arm a miniature javelin,
            throwing plastic
into the sea

Pebbles
      filling its throat

The ocean keeps swallowing
                over and over
Isn't the sea forever?

The body washed dark

       A tree of naked branches
holding the same lone crow
every evening on the same bare limb
the way a pair of lungs holds a packet of air
         in its upper reaches
               the erratic black flap of it
clattering baggily among the shadows,
and the barren ground beyond the gate
absorbs the slow drizzle
           that will deepen to rain
and your iron door creaks and clicks
into the slow-turning shortening days
your bird-heart momentarily opening
its red beak
to let
         out
a quill of crackled notes

Immersion

> *Ubi amoribi dolor*
> —Anon

Liquid slowly
webs my fingers and toes,
    then it's the spiralling

dance
              down
   down
      to the house
of algae-curtained rock and silt,
diatoms pulsing
between my teeth,
through the strands of my hair,
around my legs – locating every space
where breath might exist –
and there's still time to leave
behind all the broken plates,
the shouting, slamming
                      doors
and I know, I know,
you were only venting,

but look where it's led,
>	back
>	as always
>	to where
the fish become leaves
like an underwater autumn,
bedded brown mulch...

And the sinking,   the sinking

Tumbling

Words swirl
in little whirlwinds on the page
Even when they're behaving, I feel
as though I'm gazing at some
complicated log of random numbers

Enough of this, I say aloud,
                take to the beach

But there I find fish tumbling from the sky,
myself face up in a clump of seaweed,
foamy wavelets eddying about me

Blinding, this light,
different from what I'm used to –
      am I dreaming?
Back in the southern hemisphere?

Mackerel flapping on my belly

A girl, fifteen or so
standing, mouth ajar, saying nothing

I want to reach a hand, see if I can touch her
but suddenly she's not there,
       and I come to,
still lying in damp sand like a heavy log

There's nothing for it but to roll my body over,
               watch the tide
filling up the groove

Something like air

The fog comes in on little cat feet
– Carl Sandburg

The days slip by underfoot,
            like light
in mid-winter,
       and I'm taken back
to a different city, talking to myself
in another anonymous room

Feel as though I've been lunging
at the wrong things all my life, unhooking –
oh never mind
            There's so much
I want to say
     before it's all over

the place and in various registers,
always, of course,
            about that vice
of most romantics,
       collapsing, tragic,
trudging up some narrow stairs

as though in a Hitchcock movie
Or maybe not
            I watch a couple
ambling near some kind of obelisk,
       longing to touch,
try a relationship even

Catullus would be curious about
Well, why not
          We all need a wow,
to dream
     of what we can do when
we're not dreaming

There's so much
time and none, something like air, a lack
The fog comes first
         Much later, across
the waters of the possible,
    who knows,
the sun might burn   everything   clear

Selected Poetry Titles Published by SurVision Books

Contemporary Tangential Surrealist Poetry: An Anthology
Edited by Tony Kitt
ISBN 978-1-912963-44-7

Invasion: An Anthology of Ukrainian Poetry about the War
Edited by Tony Kitt
ISBN 978-1-912963-32-4

Helen Ivory. *Maps of the Abandoned City*
(New Poetics: England)
ISBN 978-1-912963-04-1

Tony Kitt. *The Magic Phlute*
(New Poetics: Ireland)
ISBN 978-1-912963-08-9

John W. Sexton. *Inverted Night*
(New Poetics: Ireland)
ISBN 978-1-912963-05-8

Afric McGlinchey. *Invisible Insane*
(New Poetics: Ireland)
ISBN 978-1-9995903-3-8

Matthew Geden. *Fruit*
(New Poetics: Ireland)
ISBN 978-1-912963-16-4

Ciaran O'Driscoll. *Angel Hour*
ISBN 978-1-912963-27-0

Order our books from http://survisionmagazine.com

www.ingramcontent.com/pod-product-compliance
Lightning Source LLC
Chambersburg PA
CBHW061311040426
42444CB00010B/2587